WILD BIRDS OF PREY!

FALCONS

By Deborah Kops

BLACKBIRCH PRESS, INC.

WOODBRIDGE, CONNECTICUT

Published by Blackbirch Press, Inc.
260 Amity Road
Woodbridge, CT 06525

Email: staff@blackbirch.com
Web site: www.blackbirch.com

©2000 by Blackbirch Press, Inc.
First Edition

3 1969 01415 9304

Dedication
For my mother,
Dina Kops,
with love

—DK

Printed in the United States

10 9 8 7 6 5 4 3 2 1

Photo Credits: Cover: ©Corel Corporation; pages 4, 5, 8, 11, 12, 14, 15, 22, 23: ©Corel Corporation; pages 6, 7, 16: ©Rick Kline/Cornell Ornithology; page 9: ©Lee Kuhn/Cornell Ornithology; page 10: ©James Weaver/Cornell Ornithology; page 13: ©Ralph Ginzberg/Peter Arnold; page 17: ©Arthus Bertrand/Peter Arnold; page 18: ©S & W Spofford/Cornell Ornithology; page 19: ©Digital Stock; page 20: ©Mike Hopiak/Cornell Ornithology; page 21: ©Dwight Long/Cornell Ornithology.

Library of Congress Cataloging-in-Publication Data
Kops, Deborah.
  Falcons / by Deborah Kops
      p.   cm. — (Wild birds of prey)
  Includes bibliographical references.
  Summary: An introduction to various species of falcons, describing their physical characteristics, feeding habits, parental behavior, and more.
  ISBN 1-56711-272-2
  1. Falcons—Juvenile literature. [1. Falcons.] I. Title II. Series.
QL696.F34K66   2000
598.9′44—dc21   99-046276
                                                              CIP

Contents

Introduction

Falcons live in most regions of North America, nesting in woodlands, prairies, and even in cities. If you live in a large city, you may have experienced the thrill of watching a peregrine chase down a pigeon. It takes off from a tall building or bridge in a breathtaking dive. Then it swoops down on the startled pigeon and grabs it in midair with its sharp talons.

Falcons can be found in many North American habitats.

Falcons are slender, long-winged birds of prey. They belong to a group called raptors, which also includes eagles, osprey, hawks, vultures, and owls. These birds of prey eat other animals and share a number of traits that set them apart from other birds. They have strong, hooked beaks for tearing meat. And they have sharp, curved claws, called talons, for catching and grasping their victims. Birds of prey are some of the best winged hunters in the world, and falcons are among the most exciting to watch.

Falcons, like other birds of prey, are powerful hunters and excellent fliers.

Members of the Family

Humans have admired falcons for thousands of years. Ancient Egyptians worshipped Horus, a falcon-headed god. They even kept falcon mummies; about 800,000 were found buried near a temple. Egyptians were also one of the first people to practice the sport of falconry—using falcons and other raptors to catch game animals.

Kestrels are the smallest members of the falcon family.

Today there are more than 50 species (kinds) of falcons around the world. Six of them breed in North America. One member of the falcon family—the crested caracara—is not a true falcon. It is larger and acts more like a vulture.

American Kestrel

Kestrels are the smallest falcons, about the size of robins. Like most North American falcons, kestrels may migrate (change locations seasonally). Those that live in Canada migrate south for the winter.

Some kestrels living in the United States remain there year-round. Kestrels live in a variety of habitats, from the grasslands of the Great Plains to the busy streets of East-Coast cities.

Aplomado Falcon

Aplomados are elegant, medium-sized falcons with boldly marked faces. They are in danger of extinction, which means that they could soon die out completely. But scientists have created a program to breed and release young aplomados into the south-western United States. They hope to restore the species population.

Gyrfalcon

The largest of the falcons, this powerful hunter lives in the Arctic regions of North America. A female gyrfalcon is more than twice the length of a female kestrel. Its wingspan, measured from the tip of one outstretched wing to the tip of the other, is more than 4 feet (1.2 meters) wide!

Gyrfalcons are the largest falcons.

Merlin

The fast-flying merlin is only a little larger than a kestrel. Many merlins breed in Canadian forests and migrate south in the winter. Others live on the flat northern plains of the United States year-round, where some have been known to settle in cities.

Peregrine Falcon

This graceful flier and powerful hunter breeds on every continent except Antarctica. In North America, the 16-inch- (40 centimeter) long peregrine has adapted to a variety of habitats. It inhabits everything from icy tundra to desert mountains. Some even nest in cities. Adaptability has helped save the peregrine falcon from extinction in North America.

Merlins are slightly larger than kestrels and are fast fliers.

Peregrine falcons are excellent hunters that can adapt well to many different environments.

Prairie Falcon

A prairie falcon is about the same size as a peregrine. It nests in the dry, open country of the western United States. In winter, some prairie falcons migrate a short distance and are seen hunting in cities or on farms.

Crested Caracara

A crested caracara is chunkier than a falcon. It has longer legs, and a striking black crest on its head. Its slow flight and its habit of scavenging for dead animals makes it seem most like a vulture. Because of these similar habits, the two birds often compete for food. Caracaras are year-round residents of Florida, Texas, and Arizona.

The crested caracara is marked by a unique black crest on its head.

The Body of a Falcon

Long, broad wings and a streamlined body shape make falcons fast fliers.

A falcon's long, pointed wings and tail give the bird a streamlined shape with little wind resistance. This shape is ideal for fast flying. A peregrine can dive at a speed up to 175 miles (281 kilometers) per hour, which is unmatched by any raptor. In comparison, a diving golden eagle has been recorded at a speed of 120 miles (193 kilometers) per hour.

A crested caracara's wings are shaped differently from a falcon's. They are broader and less pointed, which is perfect for slow flight at low altitudes.

Falcons don't have very colorful plumage (feathers). Most are some combination of black, gray, brown, or white. Falcons of the same species may be different colors, depending on where they live. For example, most gyrfalcons that live in northeastern Canada are white, but those in the eastern province of Labrador are gray. Although these variations in color are called phases, the birds remain the same color throughout their lives.

In contrast to its plumage, a raptor's face may have small patches of colorful skin. Peregrines, gyrfalcons, and merlins have yellow bands around their eyes, called eye-rings. Crested caracaras have orange-colored skin between their beaks and their eyes. When they are excited, the skin turns yellow.

Like most raptors, female falcons are larger than males. In some falcon species, this size difference is very striking. A female prairie falcon, for example, is one-third larger than her mate!

Top: Many falcons have yellow bands around their eyes, called eye-rings.
Above: Crested caracaras—like all raptors—have sharp, pointed beaks for tearing apart prey.

11

Special Features

In order to find their prey, falcons depend on their excellent eyesight. A kestrel hovering high over a field can even see mouse urine! This lets the bird know that its prey is nearby.

Super-sharp eyesight is key to a falcon's hunting success.

Birds of prey all have long, sharp talons that grip prey and hold it well during flight.

City Peregrines

Most North American peregrines live on cliffs along coastlines, rivers, and lakes. During the last century, however, sprawling urban areas have replaced much of the peregrine's habitats. In the 1940s, a famous pair of falcons in Montreal nested on a skyscraper. It offered an excellent view of the tasty pigeons below, and predators could not reach them. For the next 20 years, the female continued to lay her eggs and raise her families there. About a decade later, when North American peregrines came close to extinction, scientists

began breeding the birds in captivity. Since there was a shortage of good peregrine habitats in the East, scientists followed the example of the Montreal peregrines and released some of the young in cities.

The releases were a huge success. A total of 12 pairs of peregrines nest in New York City. One pair lives on the stone towers of the Brooklyn Bridge. Others make their home behind a gargoyle on the huge Riverside Church. And there are many others at choice locations throughout the city.

Once it sees its prey, a falcon uses its long toes and needle-sharp talons to grasp it. But unlike other raptors, falcons often kill their prey with their beaks, instead of their talons. Falcons have deep notches in their upper beaks. This enables them to cut through their prey's spinal cord—a vitally important cord of nerve tissue. Once the spinal cord has been severed, the prey dies.

Hunting

A crested caracara is known to eat what it can find most easily. Early in the morning, this bird sometimes patrols the highways, looking for animals that were killed by cars. If a vulture has found one first, the caracara might threaten the other bird and force it to regurgitate, or vomit, what it has eaten. The caracara will then eat the partially digested food.

Once prey is spotted, falcons will swoop down and attack quickly.

True falcons prefer to hunt live birds. To do this, they often pick a high perch to survey their territory. Merlins are experts at hunting in the air. Once one spies a meal, it begins a high-speed chase. A merlin can keep up with the fastest birds, including swifts, which can fly 100 miles (161 kilometers) per hour. A merlin can also turn quickly, reversing direction, forcing a small bird to fly too high. At that point, the small bird falls down—right into the talons of the hungry merlin.

Left: A peregrine cloaks, or hides, its prey from enemies.
Above: Hunting perches provide a clear view of the surroundings from high above.

Gyrfalcons sometimes pursue their prey over great distances. Kestrels chase birds and dragonflies in the air, but also hover over fields, in search of mice. Aplomado falcons sometimes hunt in pairs. This doubles their chances of catching a dove or a bat.

Peregrines are masters at diving and swooping. They can also zoom up to a bird, flip over, and grab it with their talons.

Despite their skill, falcons miss more prey than they catch. But one peregrine, nicknamed "the Red Baron," had an astonishing hunting record on the coast of New Jersey. Over the course of 44 days, it made 68 successful kills and did not lose its prey even once!

The Food Supply

The diet of a prairie falcon varies according to the season. It eats squirrels in early summer, and songbirds in winter.

Peregrines and merlins are widely distributed across North America, and their diet depends on where they live. In urban areas, for example, merlins

A kestrel dines on a worm.

Prairie falcons hunt small mammals and other birds for their main sources of food.

The Ancient Art of Falconry

Thousands of years ago, Egyptians, Chinese, and Persians (now called Iraqis) trained falcons and other raptors to hunt and kill wild game for them. The sport of falconry became very popular in Asia and Europe. During the Middle Ages, (A.D. 500 to 1500), members of each social class in Europe were assigned a certain raptor. Kings flew gyrfalcons, for example,

and servants flew goshawks. Today, enthusiastic falconers continue to practice this ancient sport. They enjoy the close partnership they develop with their birds during the long process of training them. Instead of taking them from the wild, however, many falconers choose birds that were raised in special breeding programs.

eat house sparrows, while peregrines eat pigeons. Near a coastline, a peregrine will hunt large seabirds, such as geese. A coastal merlin will chase small shore birds. One merlin that spent a winter along the Pacific coast consumed a total of 138 sandpipers and an assortment of other small birds!

Gyrfalcons eat the birds and mammals that are found in the far north, including hares and geese. When prey is scarce, they will adjust by skipping a breeding season to conserve food.

Mating and Nesting

In order to attract a mate for the breeding season, birds perform showy rituals called courtship displays. Crested caracaras often preen, or groom, one another. Their falcon relatives, however, usually take to the air. Male merlins put on spectacular displays that include steep dives and smooth glides. Prairie falcons give thrilling acrobatic performances near their nesting ledges.

A male and female nesting pair of merlins. Males use a showy flying display to attract their mates.

Gyrfalcons look for nests that have been built by other birds.

When they are ready to nest, most falcon pairs look for a secure place high above the ground. They don't actually build a nest, however. Kestrels use hollow trees that used to belong to other hole-nesting birds. Peregrines and prairie falcons like rocky ledges, where they push together loose sand or gravel to form a scrape. Gyrfalcons lay eggs on ledges, too, but instead of making a scrape, they look for a nest that has been built by some other bird, such as a golden eagle.

The female falcon usually lays 3 or 4 eggs and sits on them for about a month to keep them warm. This process is called incubation. The male provides the female with food. Among some species, such as kestrels, males also help incubate the eggs. Kestrels and crested caracaras sometimes have a second batch of eggs after the first group of young has grown.

Raising Young

When a falcon chick is ready to hatch, it begins to push against its eggshell. It also calls to its mother, who encourages it by calling back. After hours—sometimes even days—the chick pecks free of its shell. It emerges with its eyes closed, and is covered with a thin layer of soft feathers called down.

A peregrine chick is covered in soft down.

During the first few weeks, the female stays with the helpless chicks while the male hunts for food to feed the family. Usually, he gives his prey to the female, who feeds the chicks. If the food isn't needed right away, the male may hide it for later. Most male falcons cache, or hide, food during the breeding season. Kestrels have been known to stash their prey in everything from rain gutters to the tops of utility poles.

As it grows larger, a young falcon's flight feathers start to come in. At first, they stick up at odd angles between the soft down. When the falcon gets closer to fledging, or taking its first flight, it may hop up and down at the edge of its nest as if practicing for takeoff. Small falcons such as kestrels fledge a month or so after hatching. Gyrfalcons and peregrines need about an extra 2 weeks.

After the young fledge, falcon parents will feed them for another few weeks, until they learn how to hunt for themselves. Like most young birds, many are killed by predators, or have fatal accidents. Falcons that survive to adulthood live an average of 10 years.

A nest full of gyrfalcons that are nearly ready to fledge (leave the nest for the first time).

Falcons and Humans

The peregrine falcon nearly became extinct in North America.

Although humans had been taking over more and more of peregrines' habitat, the population remained healthy until the 1950s. That's when farmers and lumber companies began spraying crops and trees with DDT. This poisonous chemical was intended to kill harmful insects, but it also polluted the peregrines' habitats and poisoned their food.
By 1964, scientists were shocked to discover that there was not one pair of breeding peregrines in the eastern United States.

Because of harmful human activities in the 1950s, peregrine falcons nearly became extinct.

In all of North America, there were only 324 birds left. DDT was eventually banned in the United States and Canada. But that was not enough to save the peregrines.

Falcons and other birds of prey can only survive if humans do not threaten their habitats.

To boost the population, scientists came up with a plan. They decided to breed falcon pairs under close supervision. Then they took the chicks to an appropriate release site, such as a cliff or rocky ledge. The chicks stayed in a wooden box called a hack box, where they were fed by humans and could look out at their surroundings. When they were ready to fledge, the front of the box was opened.

Peregrines have been "hacked out" in the Grand Canyon, on coastal marshes, and in cities. In North America, there are now more than 1,600 breeding pairs of peregrine falcons, which are no longer in danger of extinction. The pioneering technique used to save them has also helped bald eagles, aplomado falcons, and osprey.

Glossary

habitat The place and natural conditions in which a plant or animal lives.

incubation Keeping eggs warm until they hatch.

migrate To temporarily change locations at a certain time of year.

regurgitate To bring back from the stomach to the mouth.

species One of the groups that animals and plants are divided into according to their shared characteristics.

tundra A cold, treeless area where the ground under the topsoil is permanently frozen.

For More Information

Books

Fourie, Denise. Frank Balthis (Photographer). *Hawks, Owls, and Other Birds of Prey*. Morristown, NJ: Silver Burdett Press, 1995.

Latimer, Johnathan. Karen Stray Nolting. Roger Tory Peterson (Illustrator). *Birds of Prey* (Peterson Field Guides for Young Naturalists). Boston, MA: Houghton Mifflin Co., 1999.

Wenngren, Andrew. *Who's For Dinner?: Predators and Prey* (Animal Planet). New York, NY: Crown Publishing, 1998.

Web Site

Peregrine Falcons in Acadia
www.acadia.net/anp/w95026ao.html
Learn the history, conservation, and development of falcons in this national park.

Index